THE KELVEDON TO TOLLESBURY l
A Pictorial History

FOREWORD

This mainly pictorial history of the Kelvedon & Tollesbury railway has been published to conincide with the 50th anniversary of the final closure of the branch line. England once had a plethora of rural branch lines, many of which meandered across the countryside, and led a quiet uneventful life. Some of them were uneconomic from the day they were built, but with the inexorable growth of road transport taking away their traffic - both freight and passenger - others similarly became uneconomic, with the vast majority succumbing to closure.

Essex had many branch lines: those to Brightlingsea, Maldon and Thaxted are all but memories. Thankfully, some have remained open to this day, such as the branch line to Southminster. These lines all had individual characteristics, and many of them are fondly remembered by older folk and railway enthusiasts alike.

The Kelvedon and Tollesbury had a relatively short life: the line beyond Tollesbury to the Pier lasted just a few years, whilst the main section enjoyed a passenger service for just forty seven years. Goods traffic survived in ever decreasing quantities for another eleven years.

I would like to thank the following people for their assistance in producing this book: John D. Mann, G. R. Mortimer, Brian Pask, Brian Stephenson, Alan Sermons, Ron Sargent and Peter Bugg. In addition, thanks to all the photographers, who are individually credited.

Mark House

First pu1blished 2013
Copyright East Anglian Railway Museum
Designed and published by East Anglian Railway Museum Publications
ISBN 978-0-9553121-6-8
British Library Cataloguing in Publication Data
A catalogue record for this book is available from the British Library

Printed by the Crescent Card Company, Tiptree, Colchester, Essex

£4.95

CHAPTER ONE: THE FORMATIVE YEARS

England today has an extensive road system, with a network of motorways and dual carriageways. Many towns and villages are by-passed the interests of providing fast journeys, and there is a steady stream of lorries along all the main roads. When this is compared with the Victori era a very different picture emerges. Road transport then was still horse drawn, and virtually every town and village was served by a railway li which was the prime mover for both freight and passenger traffic.

However, even in the latter days of the Victorian era there were smaller places that were not linked into the railway system, relying inste on horse drawn transport to connect them to the nearest stations. This put these locations at a decided disadvantage, particularly when it came trade. The 1890s were a period of economic downturn, and one of the schemes promoted by the government was to try and support increas business activity. The passing in 1896 of the Light Railways Act was one such measure.

This Act provided some financial assistance for the construction of lines in the more rural areas, particularly where there was insufficie traffic likely to make the lines commercially viable, or where the rate of financial return would be insufficient to make them attractive to t shareholders of the main railway companies. These lines could be built more cheaply as they generally followed more closely the contours of t countryside, with no major earthworks, bridges or tunnels. They were operated at a lower speed, which meant that level crossings often were of t open style, without the need - and cost - of staff to operate crossings. The Kelvedon & Tollesbury Light Railway was a prime example.

The area to the east of Kelvedon - which had itself gained a railway in 1843 and situated on the main London to Colchester road, an area w no rail communication, spreading across to the River Blackwater and the Essex coast, with no major ports. The farmland, however, was of gc quality - but the roads to the stations were very poor, and often impassable in prolonged periods of wet weather due to mud. Local farmers w wished to send their produce to the great London markets had to use horse drawn traffic to the nearest railheads - Kelvedon, Witham and Malc - where goods had to be manually transhipped on to trains. In terms of both finance and speed of reaching their markets, this put local farmers a disadvantage.

In 1895, Sir William Abdy, Lord of Barn Hall Manor at Tolleshunt Knights, persuaded a number of his fellow landowners in the area to don the land needed to build a line through it. Naturally, Sir William would have benefited himself - as would the others involved. He met with inconsiderable success, with around half of the land needed being donated free of charge.

With the Light Railways Act being passed in 1896, this encouraged local people to make an application for a Light Railway Order in May 18 This was for a line of nine miles six furlongs seven chains in length from Kelvedon to a terminus on the shore of the River Blackwater. The f promoters of the line were the aforementioned Sir William Abdy, together with Alex McMullen (a local landowner and Mayor of Hertford), John Sal James Paxman and Arthur C. Wilkin. The last named was the owner of the Britannia Fruit Preserving Company of Tiptree, which survives to this and now bears the Wilkin name. In May 1898 the Lands Commission of the Treasury promised to provide a £16.000 grant when the line v completed, subject to two principal conditions being met. These were that all the land needed for the railway was to be provided free of charge the landowners, and that the line was to be operated by the Great Eastern Railway. Discussions had already been held with the Great Eastern Rail who had agreed - after lengthy negotiations - to operate the line when built, so this was not a problem. A fund was established to provide the fu to purchase the land which had not already been donated: of the £650 required, Sir William Abdy and Mr McMullen provided almost half.

On 25th October 1898 a public enquiry was held in Kelvedon to consider the plans for the line. Sir William Abdy said that the 9ƒ mile li which would be standard gauge and steam operated, was to follow a route passing through the villages of Inworth, Tiptree, Tolleshunt Knigh lleshunt D'Arcy and Tollesbury. From there, it was planned to extend the line to Mill Creek on the River Blackwater. Here, the river estuary was er 1° miles wide, and the railway was planned to terminate on a long pier which was to be over ˘ mile long, meaning it would be accessible by ter at all states of the tide. The total cost of the line was estimated at £45,500 or £4,667 per mile.

The main London to Colchester road at Feering and two minor roads at Tolleshunt Knights were planned to have overbridges, and another road at leshunt Knights was to have an underbridge. Other smaller lightly used roads were to have a total of fifteen gated level crossings. However, when the e was completed there was actually just one overbridge, no underbridge and a total of nineteen level crossings, just five of which were gated. mission was given to run mixed trains, and these did not have to be fitted with continuous brakes. There was no significant opposition to the plans: ex County Council required the line to be fully fenced, and Maldon Rural District Council unsuccessfully wanted all the level crossings manned.

Following this local enquiry, application was then made to the Board of Trade, when there was a further enquiry on 16th March 1899, chaired Sir Courtenay Boyle. The promoters were represented by Mr Frere and Mr A.C. Wilkinson. The General Manager of the Great Eastern Railway, Sir liam Birt, appeared to lend the support of the GER. The only objection was against the ruling that all trains had to slow down to 10 mph within) yards of all level crossings. In due course, on 29th January 1901, the line was authorised under a Light Railway Order: when this was confirmed 27th February 1901 the 10mph restriction only applied within 200 yards of the level crossings.

The contract for the building of the line was awarded to London based firm of Scott Middleton. On 11th November 1902 there was a emonial cutting of the first sod at Feering. At its peak, over two hundred men were involved in the construction of the line. As with most other ways, the earth used for embankments came from excavations for the one cutting on the line. The one overbridge was at Blind Lane, Tolleshunt ghts. The GER influence is shown by the line's engineer being Mr A. E. Wilson, who was the son of the GER's Chief Engineer. Scott Middleton pointed Mr P. Riach as their engineer.

It was originally planned that the line should be completed by summer 1904, but the winter of 1903 was exceptionally wet which caused ificant problems with earthworks. The opening eventually on 1st October 1904 was without any special ceremony taking place. This day too was rked with wet weather, which failed to dampen the enthusiasm of the one hundred and twenty guests.

The special first train left Kelvedon at 11am and at Tiptree workers from the jam factory greeted the train as it passed on its way to lesbury, which was reached without any problems. On arrival a number of curious but enthusiastic villagers were in attendance. Alighting at lesbury, the guests proceeded to the River Blackwater, probably following the line of the then incomplete Pier extension. Fortuitously, the ather had by then improved somewhat with sunny intervals, and the guests returned to the King's Head hostelry for luncheon. This was the only lding specially decorated for the opening day's ceremony. After their repast, the guests assembled and joined the train for the return journey to vedon. Some of the villagers took the opportunity to have their first train trip.

Work continued apace on the Pier extension, but it was not completed for over two and a half years, with the official opening ceremony ing place on 15th May 1907. Grandiose plans were put forward for the pier, with - amongst other developments - new housing and a yacht station nned, together with the idea of boats to the continent. These plans, however, were never to develop.

The line then settled down to a steady if unspectacular existence for the next few years. The outbreak of the first World War brought litional traffic to the line, with more produce sent to London to make up for a lack of imported foodstuffs, together with some troop training ing place near Tollesbury. There were no cutbacks in the branch train service: in the latter part of the War an additional train each way added. er the war ended, the first road competition appeared in 1919 when a local garage proprietor, Osborne, began running buses in the area, viding new links such as a direct service to Colchester, which obviated the need to change trains at Kelvedon.

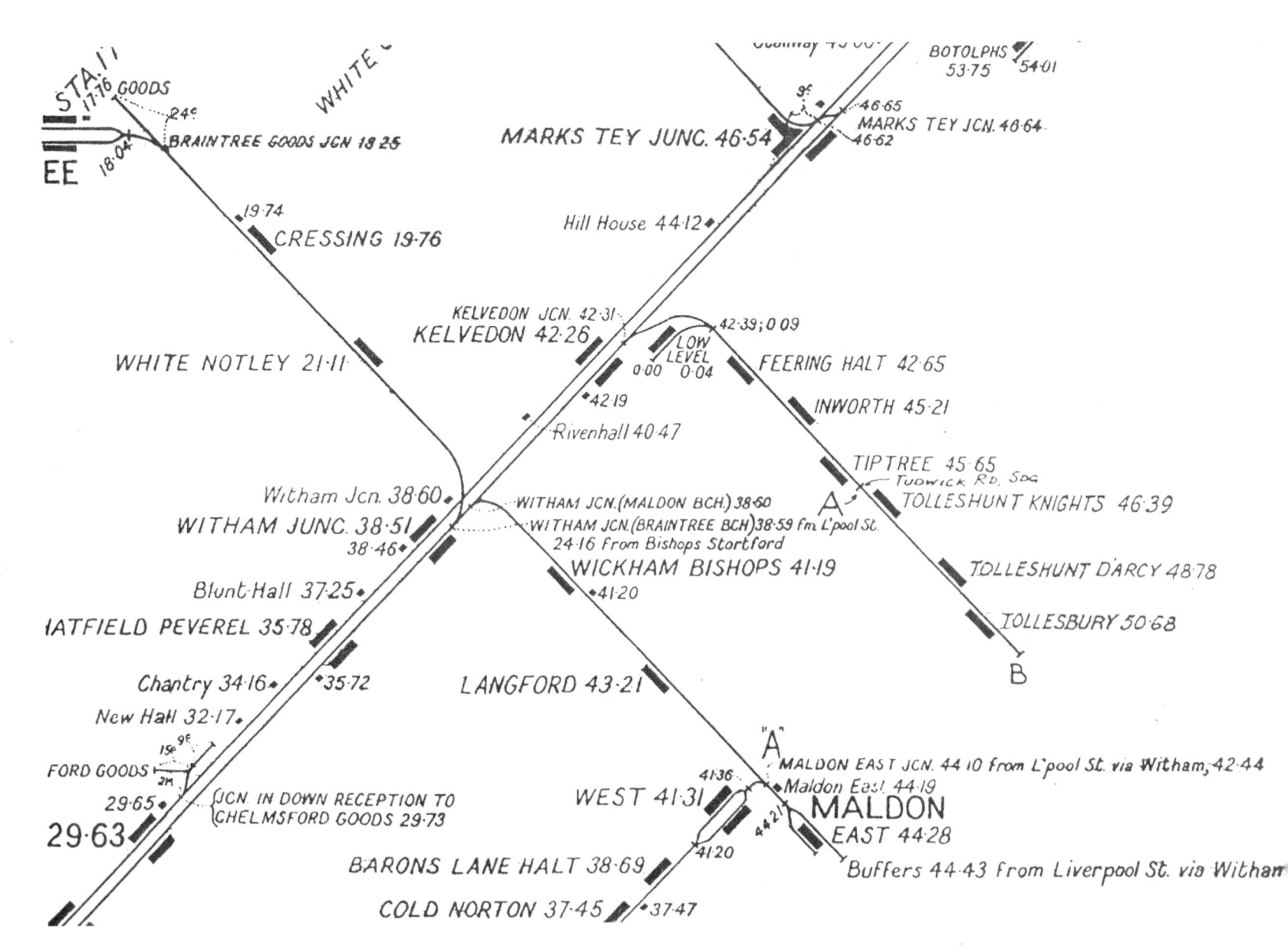

STA. 17.76 GOODS
24c
18.04
EE
BRAINTREE GOODS JCN. 18.25
19.74
CRESSING 19.76
WHITE
Gainsway 45·00
BOTOLPHS 53.75 54·01
9c
46·65
MARKS TEY JUNC. 46·54
MARKS TEY JCN. 46.64
46·62
Hill House 44·12

KELVEDON JCN. 42·31
KELVEDON 42·26
42·39; 0·09
LOW LEVEL 0·04
0·00
FEERING HALT 42·65
INWORTH 45·21
WHITE NOTLEY 21·11
42·19
Rivenhall 40·47
TIPTREE 45·65
Tudwick Rd. Sdg
TOLLESHUNT KNIGHTS 46·39
Witham Jcn. 38·60
WITHAM JCN. (MALDON BCH.) 38·60
WITHAM JUNC. 38·51
WITHAM JCN. (BRAINTREE BCH.) 38·59 fm L'pool St.
38·46
24·16 from Bishops Stortford
TOLLESHUNT D'ARCY 48·78
Blunt Hall 37·25
WICKHAM BISHOPS 41·19
41·20
TOLLESBURY 50·68
HATFIELD PEVEREL 35·78
B
Chantry 34·16   35·72
LANGFORD 43·21
New Hall 32·17
"A"
15c 9c
2M
FORD GOODS
MALDON EAST JCN. 44·10 from L'pool St. via Witham, 42·44
41·36
Maldon East 44·19
29·65
WEST 41·31
44·21
MALDON
JCN. IN DOWN RECEPTION TO CHELMSFORD GOODS 29·73
EAST 44·28
29·63
41·20
Buffers 44·43 from Liverpool St. via Witham
BARONS LANE HALT 38·69
COLD NORTON 37·45   37·47

common with many other areas, men returning from war service had been introduced to road transport. Army surplus lorries were available at very cheap prices, often being able to undercut the railway. Buses too became more available and with the gradual development of more reliable vehicles these too had an effect on the branch. The short lived General Strike of 1919 was followed by the longer, more famous one of 1926, which forced many people to look at alternative means of transportation, both for themselves and their produce. In some cases it was easier to take the produce directly to the main line railhead, or, indeed, direct to the destination. Plans for the Pier area came to nothing, and as such the Pier extension was an early casualty, closing to passengers on 17th July 1921, after a life of just fourteen years.

With the amalgamation of the railways in 1923, the line became part of the larger London & North Eastern Railway. This meant little immediate change, and whilst some East Anglian branch lines lost their passenger service in the 1930s (such as Bentley to Hadleigh and Mellis to Eye) the Kelvedon Tollesbury line was spared. In an effort to increase passenger numbers, a new halt was opened at Feering on 1st January 1934. Life continued at its slow but steady pace until the Second World War in 1939. Shortly after the outbreak of war the service was reduced to just two passenger and one freight train per day. There was, however, some increase in passenger numbers during the war due to petrol rationing cutting back the number of buses.

World War II came to the branch on Monday 9th September 1940 with the arrival of a Royal Engineers detachment to prepare firing positions for four rail-mounted guns which the War Office had decided to station at Tollesbury.

The four guns were sited on the Pier extension, two adjacent to the Woodroffe Road crossing and the others are believed to be by the lane crossing to Tollesbury Wick. Preparatory work required included re-sleepering and ballasting, and building up the formation to provide a firm foundation for the timber baulks that in turn supported the outrigger girders of the gun trucks. In addition, there were twenty two other vehicles, for ammunition, stores, workshop facilities and messing and sleeping facilities. Two ex-GWR Dean Goods 0-6-0s locomotives - manned by Royal Engineers – were provided for these.

Whilst these vehicles were within the maximum axle loading for the branch, they were by far the heaviest vehicles that were normally used and would have caused some strain on the lightly laid track. The support vehicles included Continental ferry vans and bogie coaches. With additional agricultural traffic due to the need to replace imports, regular shunting was required to enable the branch to operate. On 12th January 1941 during shunting operations both locomotives were derailed. By July 1941 the guns were deemed to be of better use elsewhere, and were moved to new locations.

CHAPTER TWO: CLOSURE OF THE LINE

With peace returning, road traffic once more increased to the detriment of the branch line, and by 1947 passenger numbers were down to an average of 67 journeys a day. Ancient rolling stock with down at heel locomotives which had suffered from neglect during the war years gave little encouragement to potential passengers. Nationalisation of the railways took place in 1948, and in common with many other lines examination was quickly taken to see if economies could be made. Plans were submitted for the complete withdrawal of the passenger service, together with the total closure of the section between Tudwick Road siding and Tollesbury.

There was no real opposition to the plans, and in due course closure was announced as taking place from 7th May 1951. With no Sunday train services, this meant that the last passenger trains would run on Saturday 5th May 1951. One week prior to this, the line played host to a special train organised by the Railway Club of Great Britain.

On the last day of service, over four hundred people turned up at Kelvedon wanting a last ride on the branch line. The branch locomotive for the day was J69/1 No. 60570, and was immaculately turned out and its coaches suitably decorated. The last train had Maldon's MP, Tom Driberg, on the footplate as honorary fireman for the day, and when it departed from Kelvedon it was to a cacophony of fog detonators, football rattles and gene cheering. More people boarded at the intermediate stations with around 450 people packed into the three coaches. At Tiptree, a black coffin had been p on the platform with wreaths covering it, one of the wreaths being in the shape of the letters 'BR'. Chalked on the smokebox of the locomotive was 'Bo 1904 Died 1951', whilst similarly chalked on the bunker was the warning 'there be many a poor soul have to walk'. Another rousing send-off took place Tiptree, and the train reached Tollesbury at 6.25pm, some forty minutes after leaving Kelvedon. The return journey was just as noisy before it reach Kelvedon Low Level for the last time. The coaches were left at Kelvedon, whilst the locomotive steamed off to Colchester.

The Tudwick Road siding to Tollesbury section was closed completely on 29th October 1951, with lifting of the line from Tudwick Road to t Pier being carried out soon afterwards, with most of the land being sold to local landowners. The remaining section to Tiptree and Kelvedon v kept open for freight traffic, serving the Wilkins Jam Factory and local coal merchants Garwoods and Sons.

However, keeping the line open for running freight traffic was found to be uneconomic, with losses estimated at over £600 per annum. W freight traffic being concentrated at one location in each area under BR's Modernisation Plan, this was to be handled at Maldon East with parcels Witham. With no objections to closure being received, the last freight train ran on Friday 28th September 1962, hauled by Class 05 diesel shunt locomotive number D2571: just one cyclist, watching, as the railway passed into history.

CHAPTER 3: THE ROUTE FOLLOWED

Kelvedon is well served by rail and road, with part of the trackbed of the K&T now occupied by the A12 by-pass. The station is situated on main line from Colchester to London, and until the 1960s there were small goods yards on both sides of the main line at the London end of station. The original station buildings were demolished in 1990, when the present ticket office was built. The old footbridge was replaced b concrete structure when the line was electrified.

To the north of the station on the Up side of the main line, lay the Low Level station. There was a freight only connection up a steeply grad siding. For passengers, it was necessary to walk along a footpath across the railway bridge and down a path to the Low Level platform.

The branch terminus comprised a small wooden waiting shed, as all other business was handled at the main station, and a platform whic like all others on the branch - stood only fifteen inches above rail level. Behind the platform ran the connecting line to the main line which beca of the steep gradient was used only by goods traffic. At the London end the line terminated at the engine shed, where a coal stage and water colu was provided. The branch engine was housed here overnight, returning to Colchester, its home shed, every Saturday evening for a boiler washe and other maintenance. Completing the limited facilities a weighbridge was installed to ensure that no engine with an axle load exceeding fourte tons worked on the branch, the limit imposed under the Light Railways Act.

Signals here were the only working ones on the branch, and were controlled from a small signal cabin, the warning distant near Feering be fixed. A unique set of hand-operated three-way points could also be seen in the yard. These points, as were all others on the branch, worked on Annett principle. By this system all point levers, whether controlled by hand lever or by ground-frame levers, were kept locked, and could only released by a key attached to the train staff.

Leaving Kelvedon, the branch curved sharply away from the main line, on a rising gradient of 1 in 63, passing one of the numerous crossin After just over ˇmile, run mainly through a cutting, the fixed distant was passed. A few yards further on the level crossing over the Londor Colchester road was reached: as the gates were operated by the train crew, long queues of traffic could build up here.

the Tollesbury side of the level crossing stood the first stop, Feering Halt, opened on January 1st 1934. This halt was intended to serve the village Feering, but is actually nearer to Kelvedon. The station building here was a converted single decker bus, which served as a waiting room. mediately beyond the halt was Brooklands private siding: all traces of both the halt and the siding have now disappeared.

e line now continued straight at a rising gradient of 1 in 50, and then fell at the same gradient. At the summit the line curved slightly, followed a 10mph speed restriction for an ungated level crossing over the narrow road to Tiptree Heath. The crossing was protected by cattle guards on ch side. These were a new innovation, introduced from America, when the line was built.

After five more occupation crossings and two level crossings, the line came to Heath Siding, 2 miles 62 chains from Kelvedon, and situated the Parish of Tiptree, more than two miles from Inworth village. The small goods yard consisted of a siding with crossover at each end, with a ding gauge and cart road: immediately beyond this siding stood Inworth, the second intermediate stopping place on the branch. The waiting commodation consisted of an old four-wheeled coach, which also served as a parcels office. The station was completed by a level crossing over main Maldon to Colchester Road, again with the gates operated by the train crews, at the Tiptree end of the station.

The line then ran for a half a mile to another ungated crossing in to Tiptree station, which had a fairly large goods yard with two sidings ding to Wilkins jam factory. The station buildings were fairly substantial, constructed mainly of wood, although an old coach body was in dence as a store. The station building was later converted into a goods office, from which all business on the branch was controlled after the hdrawal of passenger services in 1951, but the importance of the yard declined when the jam from the factory was sent by road to the extent t in 1961 not a single wagon was handled there.

The line now continued at a falling gradient around the back of the Jam factory to Tudwick Road, the site of an ungated crossing. At this point ding branched off to the north, in a trailing direction from Kelvedon. This was the terminus for freight services on the branch after 1951, and) yards past this point the track was taken up after the complete closure of the remaining section on to Tollesbury.

From there the line continued at a rising gradient of 1 in 50, the maximum gradient on the line, to reach Tolleshunt Knights Halt, situated on Kelvedon side of a gated level crossing over the road from Tiptree to Tolleshunt d'Arcy. The facilities consisted of the usual waiting room verted from an old coach body, two oil lamps, and nameboard.

For the next mile the line passes over undulating relief, rising and falling at 1 in 50, broken only by a short section of 1 in 60 near the only erbridge on the line. On this section was an agricultural siding, namely Church Siding, which was situated near the 5° mile post, and handled sonal pea traffic from nearby farms.

The gradients now eased slightly to 1 in 260, with breaks to 1 in 100, 1 in 70, and 1 in 80, before another gated crossing was reached. On the er side of the road- which led to Great Wigborough - stood Tolleshunt d'Arcy station. This small stopping place, which was staffed, was 6 miles chains from Kelvedon. It boasted accommodation similar to Inworth, although the waiting room was a former Great Eastern third class coach.

The remaining section of the line to Tollesbury was gently graded, except for a stretch into the terminus. It was however, sharply curved in ces and at one time the 0-6-0s working on the line had the front section of their coupling rods removed, to reduce flange wear. Before Tollesbury ther agricultural siding was passed. It was named Old Hall Siding and was 7 miles 62 chains from Kelvedon.

lesbury station, which had been the terminus of the line since the closure of the pier extension in 1921, was the only other staffed station on the . It consisted of a small goods yard complete with loading gauge and cart road, and wooden station buildings.

The line then crossed a road, still named Station Road today, by an open crossing on the other side of which was a run round loop. The ension to the pier skirted Tollesbury village and then fell steadily towards the river. En route the line crossed two roads, both of which led to the river. The 1770 foot long pier was of wooden construction. The pier terminus consisted of an old coach body and red brick hut, about forty yards from where the pier began. The track on the pier itself was removed in 1940 and a portion of the pier was blown out as an anti-invasion precaution. Part of the extension had been used previously for the storage of rolling stock, but the wooden pier had been allowed to fall into disrepair from 1921 onwards.

The old pier was finally demolished when the line was lifted in 1951, and the last traces were swept away in the great floods of 1953. Today only a few rotting stumps of timber, standing a foot or two above the mud at low tide, mark the position of the once majestic pier, the showpiece of the Kelvedon and Tollesbury branch.

CHAPTER FOUR: TRAIN SERVICES

As on most light railways, train services were never very rapid nor very frequent; in fact, as the majority of trains were mixed, and the time allowed for shunting was often unnecessarily long, the 8¾ mile journey always occupied between 31 and 65 minutes.

When the line was opened the Great Eastern Railway announced that, until February 1905, they would run four trains each way daily over the branch, leaving Kelvedon at 10.45 (mixed), 12.30, 2.45 and 5.40 pm, and from Tollesbury at 8.25, 11.40 am, 2.00 and 6.20 pm (mixed). The mixed trains were allowed forty minutes, and the passenger trains thirty two, for the journey. There would also be a special daily goods train between Kelvedon and Tiptree only. No trains ran on Sundays.

After only four months operation the service was reduced to three trains daily in each direction. The railway company were however quick in realising the traffic potentials of the branch. It was only forty miles from Liverpool Street, their London terminus, and the passenger could leave there at 8.55 or 10.55 am each morning to arrive at Kelvedon at 10.21 and 12.21 respectively. The passenger was then allowed twenty-four minutes to walk the short distance to the branch terminus before his train departed. After a comparatively rapid journey on the 'mixed' train, the passenger would arrive at Tollesbury at 11.25 am or 1.25pm respectively, exactly 2½ hours after leaving Liverpool Street. In order to return to London that night the traveller had to leave Tollesbury at 6.20. After a slow journey on the evening 'mixed' train and a long wait at Kelvedon, he would arrive at Liverpool Street at 9.06 pm, 2 hours 46 minutes later.

Summer 1913 timetable

In 1910 there were four weekday trains in each direction, of which all but the 2.45 pm down were extended to and from the Pier when required. An additional evening trip was run on Wednesdays and Fridays only. The 1922 timetable provided for trains leaving Kelvedon at 9.45, and 12.29 and 5.54 pm. They returned from Tollesbury at 8.24 am, 10.36 am, and 3.15 and 6.42 pm. The train also had to run empty to Tollesbury every morning to work the 8.24 am back to Kelvedon.

By 1937 traffic on the branch had begun to decline, largely due to competition from the parallel bus service. The timetable of that time had been increased to six Up trains and seven Down trains daily, two of which were mixed. Whenever mixed trains had no shunting to perform at stations, as was quite common. It was the practice to wait there until the time allowed for shunting had passed. The winter 1943 timetable saw departures from Kelvedon at 10.12 am and 5.46 pm, returning from Tollesbury at 8.30 am, 12.45 pm and 6.35 pm.

By 1947, traffic on the line had reached its lowest ebb; on an average day only 33 return passenger journeys were made. In 1948 British Railways took over, and were quick to appreciate the amount of money the line was losing. Early in 1950 plans were submitted for partial closure, as detailed earlier, and were subsequently accepted by the TUCC. The timetable in 1950 showed Kelvedon departures at 6.40am (empty to Tollesbury), then mixed trains at 10.10 am and 5.45 pm. Tollesbury departures were at 8.30 am, 12.50pm and 6.37 pm.

The remaining freight service carried chiefly coal traffic, amounting to approximately 2000 tons annually and mainly consigned to the local coal merchants of Frosts and Garwood's. As there was a larger demand for coal during the winter months, the timetable then provided for a freight train running daily Mondays to Fridays, whilst in summer no trains ran on Tuesdays and Thursdays. This train was worked by the Witham pilot engine, in later years usually a Hunslet diesel shunter. The diesel had a path to Kelvedon at 1.10 pm. During winter months it would shunt in the yard there until 3.30 pm when it would cross the main lines and set off on its journey to Tiptree. The train called en route at Inworth Siding and if needed continue to Tudwick Road Siding. The return journey was at about 4.35pm, depending on the amount of traffic, and was due at Kelvedon at 4.50pm.

During summer months, the train left Kelvedon yard at 1.35pm returning at 2.50pm. If there was insufficient traffic the branch trip was cancelled, and the diesel spent the time in Kelvedon Yard. As the traffic declined, branch trips became less and less frequent.

After 1951 two trains carrying passengers were run on the line, both rail tours: one was formed of goods brake vans, the other open wagons. The first, organised by the Railway Enthusiasts' Club, ran on 6th April 1957 and was hauled by J15 0-6-0 No. 65443. The second was run by the Railway Club on 27th September 1958, and was hauled by E4 2-4-0 No. 62785.

CHAPTER 5: LOCOMOTIVES AND ROLLING STOCK

For the opening of the line, six 4-wheel five compartment thirds and two 4-wheel two compartment brake thirds – built between 1877 and 1882 - were converted for use on the line. The partitions between the compartments were removed from all the carriages, which opened out the inside of the coaches. There was a central door at each end, opening out on to a drop-plate so to the guard could walk the between the carriages when the train was between stations so that he could sell tickets. With all of the platforms being only 1ft 3in above rail level, the original 3ft 6in Mansell wheels were swapped with ones of 2ft 9in diameter. In doing so, this meant the drawbar and buffer level on the headstocks had to be changed; also additional step boards were added to aid access. These additional step boards had to be removed before the coaches went on to the main line as they would be out of gauge. In the former five compartment coaches three of the five doors on each side were blanked off, whilst on the brake thirds only one door on each side was blanked off. All of this work was carried out at Stratford Works before the line opened in during 1904: these coaches continued in service until 1928. In January 1928 the Wisbech and Upwell Tramway was closed for passenger use and its nine coaches become redundant. Six of them were transferred to Kelvedon for use on the branc arriving between September 1928 and January 1929.

There were two types of coach from the Wisbech & Upwell Tramway: 4-wheeled examples that were 23ft 7 in long and numbered 6046 6, and two bogie ones 33ft 10˚in long numbered 60461-2. They were built in 1884 and 1890 respectively. They had the same 2ft 9in wheel the main difference being that they had open balconies at each end, with wrought iron railings and gates and drop plates for the guards to g between the carriages between stations. The seats were arranged along each side of the coach inside. Both the bogie coaches were original composite coaches, but when transferred to the Kelvedon & Tollesbury became open third class only. Three of the 4-wheeled tram coach were withdrawn by 1936 and the fourth in 1948: this just left the two bogie coaches that remained until passenger services were withdraw in 1951.

The Stoke Ferry branch closed to passengers in September 1930: this made redundant the line's two coaches which were one 6 wheel brake third and the other a 6 wheeled brake composite. Again they were sent to Stratford for the fitting of end doors with drop down plate and again the compartments were opened out. They also arrived in 1931 and the two original brake thirds were withdrawn.

The two ex Wisbech & Upwell bogie tram coaches and the two Stoke Ferry coaches remained in service until the Kelvedon & Tollesbu lost its passenger service. This stock was officially withdrawn later in October 1951, with coach No. 60461 being used in the film 'The Titfi Thunderbolt'. The Tollesbury branch was visited by Ealing Studios for the filming but they decided against this branch line. Coach No. 604 was restored by BR at Stratford for preservation but subsequently broken up due to an alleged lack of space. Riding on the balconies w officially forbidden but this rule often seemed to be broken: they served as great observation platforms at the end of the train.

Passengers visiting the branch always found the method utilised for fare collection and ticket issuing unusual. Firstly the guard wou go through the coaches collecting orders. He would then return to his own van and make out the tickets, which were of the bus type, print by the company's printing works at Stratford. They had the stages printed down each side, and it was the guard's duty to punch the according to the station at which the passenger boarded. When he had done this, he returned to the passengers issuing their tickets.

The first type of engine to work on the branch was a small Great Eastern class K9 0-4-2 tank: the only member of the class to work the branch was No 25. This worked the branch single handed during the first year. In 1905 it was replaced by one of Holden's R24 0-6-0 ta locomotives, which later became LNER Class J67/1. During their early years on the branch front coupling rods were removed, making them 4-0: the idea was to reduce wear and tear but this did not last for long. The J67/1s carried on working the branch but they were latterly join by members of the J68 and J69/1 classes. These two classes were officially over the maximum axle loading for the branch but were seen many occasions. The last loco used for passenger use was J69/1 No.68578. The only other locos used on the branch were the J15 0-6-0 tend locos used on ballast and breakdown trains. No.65443 worked an enthusiast's special of open trucks and brake vans on 6th April 1957. The was also one recorded visit of a E4 2-4-0 tender loco, No. 62785 (GER 490), which was used on a brake van special on 27th September 195 This loco now is now part of the National Railway Museum collection.

After the withdrawal of passenger services freight trains were either worked by the J15 or one of the tank locos, but when steam w withdrawn the only locos able to work the branch were the small Class 04 or 05 diesel locos. These two types of loco worked the branch un the freight service was withdrawn in 1962.

CHAPTER 6: AFTER CLOSURE

After the complete closure of the line from Kelvedon to Tudwick Road Siding in October 1962 little time was lost before the track was removed. Only traces are still visible to say there was once a railway. The track bed at Kelvedon Low Level is visible until it vanishes into a housing estate. At Feering Halt the only trace is a house named 'The Crossing'. The line is still partly visible until the Kelvedon bypass (A12) ploughs straight through the track bed then the line is still visible as farm tracks until it reaches Brook Sidings and Inworth station. The line from this point to Tiptree station is now built upon by housing estates and a supermarket: the only traces are a few humps in the road and a level crossing post remains. Tiptree station site is now the telephone exchange and a housing estate: beyond the land is now within the expanded jam factory which includes the site of Tudwick Road Siding. Tolleshunt Knights station is now under houses, then more houses cover the track bed through the village. Getting back in to the countryside Kind Lane bridge - the only bridge on the line - is still standing and the cutting is still visible. Further on the line becomes a farm track to Tolleshunt D'Arcy: the station house still stands, and the rest of the site is now home to some industrial units. The line after this point is a mixture of field and farm track until Tollesbury, where housing now covers all of the station site. As the village of Tollesbury has expanded more of the line has being covered up by housing. There are hardly any traces of Tollesbury Pier station and the pier apart from the odd post which can be seen can be seen at low tide but these are getting less and less now.

Tiptree has now become a large village, with many driving to Kelvedon with its easy access to the A12 or to Kelvedon Station to connect with the fast electric train service to London Liverpool Street. Many residents now would never know that there was once a line to Tiptree and beyond to Tollesbury Pier.

For a little branch line that closed to passengers before the Beeching era, some items have survived. A gas station lamp from Tiptree is now on display at Mangapps Farm Railway at Burnham-on-Crouch. The running in boards from Inworth and Tiptree and the closure poster are displayed at the East Anglian Railway Museum at Chappel & Wakes Colne Station. One of the former Wisbech and Upwell coaches now resides on the North Norfolk Railway: after many hours and much money expended on restoration it can be seen in operation on selected days.

(Right) Last day of service, with the ceremonial coffin about to be placed on the train

An elevated view of Kelvedon looking west 1911 with KTLR engine shed adjacent: the oil lit down main line platform is being extended. The covered way and path led down to the low level Kelvedon & Tollesbury platform, with the waiting room at the extreme left. (Historical Model Railway Society)

An undated view of Kelvedon Low Level station (Ken Nunn Collection, courtesy of the Locomotive Club of Great Britain)

Class J15 0-6-0 65443 on a special train of open wagons at Kelvedon main station, 6th April 1957 (N. C. Simmons, courtesy Photos Of The Fifti[es]

Class J15 0-6-0 65443 shunting the train of open wagons at Kelvedon for Tiptree, 6th April 1957
(N. C. Simmons, courtesy of Photos Of The Fifties)

Class E4 62758 at Kelvedon on a special enthusiasts train of brake vans, 27th September 1958 (The late Dr. I. C. Allen)

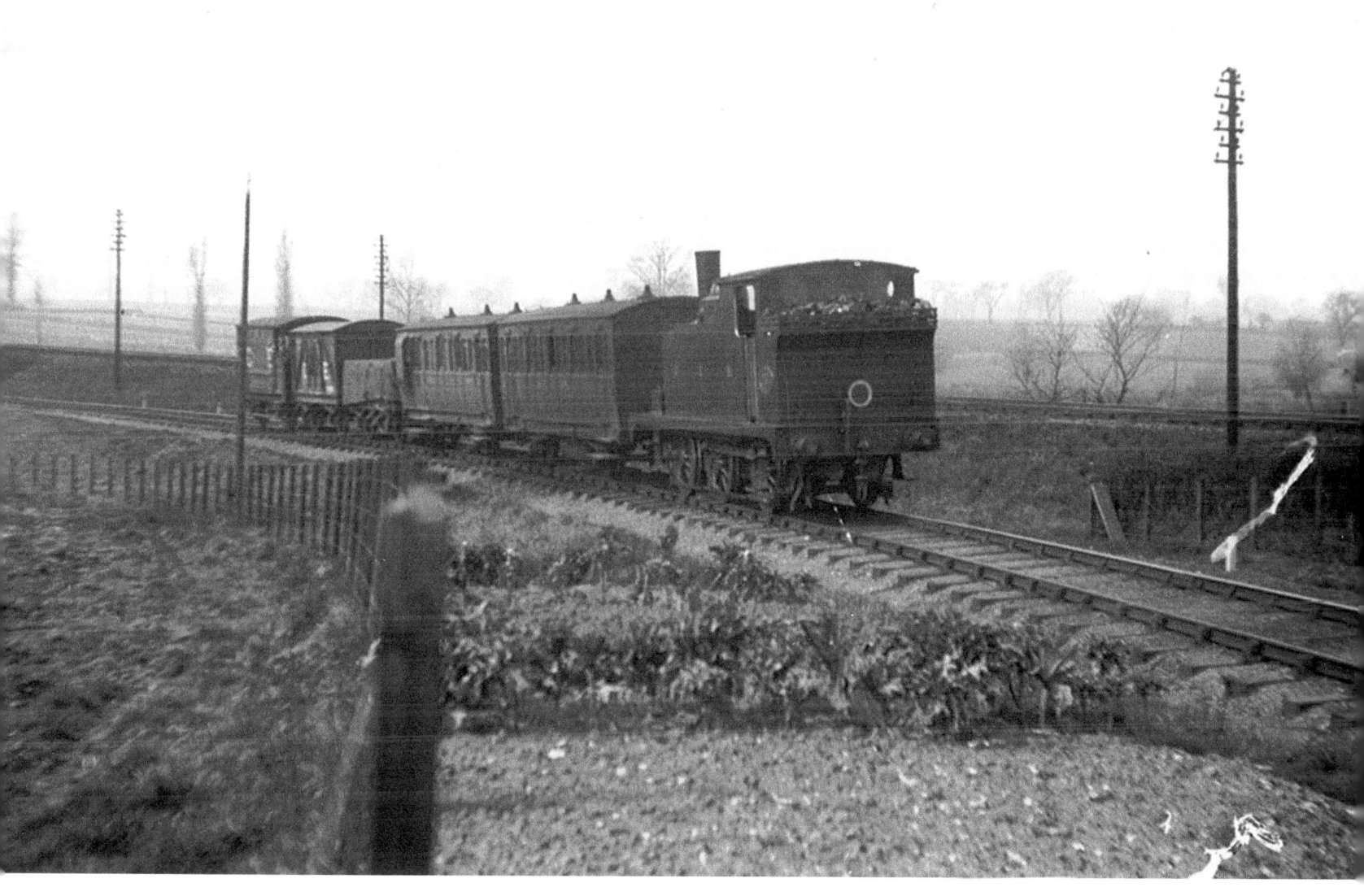

R24 No.267 departing Kelvedon with the 10.25am to Tollesbury, 9th April 1910 (Ken Nunn, courtesy Locomotive Club of Great Britain)

J67/1 68616 at Kelvedon with the 12.50pm ex Tollesbury, 29th July 1950 (Ken Nunn, courtesy of the Loocmotive Club of Great Britain)

Kelvedon Low Level station on the last day of passenger services, 5th May 1951 (JJ Smith, courtesy of the Bluebell Railway)

Coach E60462 at Kelvedon on 5th May 1951, similar to the coaches used on the Wisbech & Upwell Tramway. One of this type featured in the famous 'Titfield Thunderbolt' film (Philip J. Kelley)

J69/1 68578 taking water at Kelvedon, undated (R. E. Vincent, courtesy of The Transport Treasury)

E62261 6 wheel coach at Kelvedon Low Level 28th August 1950: note the end door corridor connection which facilitated conductor guard working (Ken Nunn, courtesy of the Locomotive Club of Great Britain)

Kelvedon Low Level on 5th May 1951: Class J69/1 68578 is about to leave for Tollesbury suitably embellished for working the last passenger train
(P. J. Kelley)

View from an open wagon of the Railway Enthusiasts Club special leaving Kelvedon, looking towards the brake van, with Kelvedon station in the distance, 6th April 1957 (Austin Attewell, courtesy of Photos Of The Fifties)

Kelvedon Low Level station on the last day of passenger services, 5th May 1951 (J. J. Smith, courtesy of the Bluebell Railway)

Interior of coach 60462, Kelvedon, 5th May 1951 (J. J. Smith, courtesy of the Bluebell Railway)

The 10.10 to Tollesbury departing Kelvedon on 28th April 1951, headed by Class J69 68578. It includes two former Stoke Ferry coaches. The final service for passengers was a week later, on 5th May 1951 (G. R. Mortimer)

Ex-LNER J15 Class (GER Y14) 0-6-0 65443 (GER 643 then LNER 7643 until 1946) leaving Kelvedon with the daily goods train to Tollesbury, 19th May 1951 (P. M. Alexander, Kidderminster Railway Museum)

Kelvedon in the diesel era, with a Class 30 diesel locomotive (later re-engined to become Class 31) passing on the Up Main. A Class 04 diesel shunter is on the low level line (Mick Smith, Ron Sargent collection)

R24 No.391 heads the 12.30pm Kelvedon to Tollesbury at the site of the future Feering Halt, 31st March 1910
(Ken Nunn, courtesy of the Locomotive Club of Great Britain)

67/1 68608 with the 12.50pm ex Tollesbury at Feering Halt, 30th September 1950 (Ken Nunn, courtesy of the Locomotive Club of Great Britain)

REC special train of open wagons at Feering Halt, passengers detraining with the aid of ladders, 6th April 1957
(Austin Attewell, courtesy of Photos Of The Fifties)

View from the brake van in the diesel era approaching Heath Siding (Mick Smith, Ron Sargent collection)

Heavily overgrown, the view after departing Feering in the diesel era (Mick Smith, Ron Sargent collection)

J15 0-6-0 65443 with the REC special train of open wagons at Feering Halt on 6 April 1957
(Brian Connell, photograph courtesy of Photos from the Fifties)

Shunting at Heath Siding, Inworth in the diesel era (Mick Smith, Ron Sargent collection)

Remains of Inworth station platform 5th March 1961, with Heath Siding in the distance (RCTS Archive - The Mallaband Collection)

LNER (ex-GER) Class J69/1 0-6-0T number 8636 at Inworth on a passenger train from Tollesbury to Kelvedon, 16th May 1949. View of station building made from ex-GER coach, station lamp and station running-in board (D. J. Powell, Kidderminster Railway Museum)

Freight train at Inworth in the diesel era with nature taking over, Ron Sargent looking back from the brake van
(Mick Smith, Ron Sargent collection)

Class J15 0-6-0 65443 with REC special train of two brake vans and three open wagons at Inworth, 6 April 1957
(D. Lawrence, courtesy of Photos Of The Fifties)

Inworth in the diesel era, with only one gate across the road due to the Permanent Way staff putting one of their trolleys through one of the gates. Note the BR poster board above the gate, still in use a decade after closure to passenger service
(Mick Smith, Ron Sargent collection)

R24 No. 267 at Tiptree on the 1.40pm Kelvedon to Tollesbury, 9th April 1910 (Ken Nunn, courtesy of the Locomotive Club of Great Britain)

J15 0-6-0 65443 with RFC special train of open wagons at Tiptree, 6th April 1957 (Austin Attewell, courtesy of Photos Of The Fifties)

Tiptree station, 27th July 1958 (Frank Church, courtesy of the Essex Bus Enthusiasts Group)

J15 65470 shunts the Tiptree Jam Factory Sidings in August 1958 (the late Dr. Ian C Allen)

Tiptree in diesel freight days: Ron Sargent standing in the doorway, Ron Humphrys, the driver, with his back to the photographer (Mick Smith, Ron Sargent collection)

Another view of an overgrown Tiptree from the diesel freight era (Mick Smith, Ron Sargent collection)

(Left) This photo from the diesel freight era is marvellously atmospheric, with Ron Humphrys driver, Derrick Jackson secondman in the cab, and Cyril Sargeant from Marks Tey acting as flagman. There were no crossing gates at Tiptree at this time.
(Mick Smith, Ron Sargent collection)

(Below) The poster announcing the withdrawal of the passenger service, now on display at the East Anglian Railway Museum

BRITISH RAILWAYS

KELVEDON AND TOLLESBURY BRANCH LINE

WITHDRAWAL OF PASSENGER TRAIN SERVICE

The Railway Executive hereby give notice that on and from Monday, 7th May, 1951 the passenger train service will be withdrawn from the undermentioned stations and halt on the Kelvedon–Tollesbury branch:—

**FEERING HALT
INWORTH
TIPTREE
TOLLESHUNT KNIGHTS
TOLLESHUNT D'ARCY
TOLLESBURY**

Parcels traffic will continue to be dealt with at Tiptree, Tolleshunt D'Arcy and Tollesbury stations until further notice.

An omnibus service operated by Messrs. Osborne & Sons is available between Tollesbury, Tiptree, Kelvedon and Witham.

The busy scene at Tiptree on the last day of passenger service (EARM collection)

Gravity shunting with Ron Sargent in charge: the brake van is about to roll forwards towards the buffer stops to release the Class 04 diesel locomotive at Tudwick Road Siding, beyond Tiptree (Mick Smith, Ron Sargent collection)

The end of the line at Tudwick Road siding, with Derek Jackson, the secondman, keeping an eye on proceedings. The use of a Class 04 diesel was a fairly rare occurrence, with Class 05 'Hunslets' predominating (Mick Smith, Ron Sargent collection)

At Tolleshunt Knights, 5th May 1951 (J. J. Smith, courtesy of the Bluebell Railway)

4 No. 267 at Blind Lane near Tolleshunt Knights on the 11.16am Tollesbury to Kelvedon, 9th April 1910: this was the only overbridge on the line (Ken Nunn, courtesy of the Locomotive Club of Great Britain)

An undated view of Tolleshunt D'Arcy station (Maldon Museum)

Tolleshunt D'Arcy in 1949; note the unusual position of the station nameboard (R. K. Blencowe)

'Stovepipe' J69 68607 at Tollesbury during the early British Railways period (the late Dr. I. C. Allen)

GER Class J15 0-6-0 No. 7567 waits to leave Tollesbury with a mixed train for Kelvedon in the 1930s
(Photo: Rail Archive Stephenson)

Where are they now? Train at Tollesbury, August 15th 1947 (the late Cyril Footer, Malcolm Root collection)

Tollesbury, August 15th 1947 - the classic 'light railway' view during the glorious summer of that year.
(The late Cyril Footer. Malcolm Root collection)

Tollesbury, August 15th 1947 (the late Cyril Footer, Malcolm Root collection)

"THERE BE MANY A POOR SOUL HAVE TO WALK"

J69/1 68578 prepares to leave Tollesbury for the last time, 5th May 1951 (K.C. Footer, J.D. Mann collection)

Class J69/1 68578 at Tollesbury, 5th May 1951 (J. J. Smith, courtesy of the Bluebell Railway)

Tollesbury, 5th May 1951 (J. J. Smith, courtesy of the Bluebell Railway)

Class J69/1 68578 at Tollesbury, 5th May 1951 (J. J. Smith, courtesy of the Bluebell Railway)

-LNER J69 class (GER R24) 0-6-0T number 68578 (GER 270 then LNER 7270 until 1946) bunker first at Tollesbury station on 5th May 1951, the
t day of passenger services. On the back of the bunker are chalked the words "There be many a poor soul have to walk" and "1904-1951" on
the side of the tank. Enthusiasts are on the tracks (P. J. Lynch, courtesy of the Kidderminster Railway Museum)

Tollesbury station looking towards Kelvedon after closure, building standing but track removed (D. Lawrence, courtesy of Photos of the Fifties)

ex-Kelvedon and Tollesbury Light Railway coaches at Tollesbury on 18th April 1949. Nearest the camera is former Wisbech & Upwell Tramway bogie coach number 60462 with a balcony at each end; this vehicle was later restored by BR but then destroyed. To the left is former GER six-wheeled coach number 62261 previously used on the Stoke Ferry branch (P. J. Lynch, courtesy of the Kidderminster Railway Museum)

After closure, coach 60462 was restored in GER livery as No.8. Seen here at Stratford on 27th January 1957. Sadly, it was subsequently scrapped
(Philip J. Kelley)